The *YOUNG WITCH'S GUIDE* *to* LIVING MAGICALLY

POTIONS, LOTIONS, RITUALS, AND SPELLS FOR KIDS

NIKKI VAN DE CAR
Illustrated by ANISA MAKHOUL

RP | KIDS
PHILADELPHIA

Recipes adapted from Emily of Layers of Happiness, Amy of She Wears Many Hats, Deb Perelman of Smitten Kitchen.

Running Press Kids
Hachette Book Group
1290 Avenue of the Americas, New York, NY 10104
www.runningpress.com/rpkids
@runningpresskids

Printed in China

First Edition: November 2023

Published by Running Press Kids, an imprint of Perseus Books, LLC, a subsidiary of Hachette Book Group, Inc. The Running Press Kids name and logo are trademarks of the Hachette Book Group.

The Hachette Speakers Bureau provides a wide range of authors for speaking events. To find out more, go to www.hachettespeakersbureau.com or email HachetteSpeakers@hbgusa.com.

Running Press books may be purchased in bulk for business, educational, or promotional use. For more information, please contact your local bookseller or the Hachette Book Group Special Markets Department at Special.Markets@hbgusa.com.

The publisher is not responsible for websites (or their content) that are not owned by the publisher.

Print book cover and interior design by Frances J. Soo Ping Chow.

Library of Congress Control Number: 2023932008

ISBNs: 978-0-7624-8401-0 (hardcover), 978-0-7624-8402-7 (ebook)

1010

10 9 8 7 6 5 4 3 2 1

CONTENTS

· ·

A NOTE ON SAFETY: This book has a lot of recipes and spells that ask you to use the stove or to chop herbs with a knife or to use ingredients that might burn or harm you if employed incorrectly. Make sure you practice your magic in a safe way and ask a parent or adult for help whenever needed—such as with a stove or knife.

WELCOME, YOUNG WITCH!

YOU ARE CHOOSING TO DO MAGIC FOR YOURSELF—THE MOST powerful witchcraft and also the simplest. Being a healthy young witch means living in harmony with the natural world and with your own creativity. And magical self-care means loving yourself and recognizing how strong you really are. Think of what your body does for you: it is the house your soul lives in, and like *Howl's Moving Castle*, it travels around with you, allowing you to live your most magical life.

Becoming a strong young witch starts with your intentions. Setting your intentions just means thinking about what you want, and it's where all magic begins. When you make something in the kitchen, whether it's a simple snack or even a full meal for your family, you can make it magical by thinking about what you're doing and being grateful for the life you take from your food. Then, you can go a little further and add some herbs—maybe for healing, happiness, or power—that can change a snack into a magic potion. You can do the same thing with potions for *outside* your body, like gentle lotions or essential oils. You can also empower your bedroom or other parts of your home to be places that soothe and inspire you.

The teas, rituals, and spells in this book are here to get you started on a wellness magic practice so that you can work with, change, and create your own spells. For instance, most potions here include instructions on whether to stir clockwise or counterclockwise. The direction you choose depends on the *kind* of potion you're making; if it's a healing potion and you want to harness the power of the sun, then you can stir clockwise, following the path of the sun and inviting its energy into your spell. Stirring counterclockwise, also known as **widdershins**, can help you find the more mysterious aspects of your magic, like when you aren't really sure what your intentions are. You can gather fresh herbs by moonlight or sunlight, or let dried herbs rest in moonlight or sunlight, which will function the same way: harnessing the bright energy of the day or unlocking the shadows of the night. If you don't have access to direct sunlight or moonlight, then you can use a lamp, a stone, or even a whispered spell, and it will work, too—because again, magic is always about what you *want* your spell to do.

You can find so much magic in making things for yourself, infusing them with your power and mystical being. This is something witches have done for centuries, and you can apply the knowledge gained through their history and traditions and combine it with your own ideas and creativity to bring peace, power, and everyday magic to your life. Wellness magic is not just something you *do*. It's a way of life that any kid can choose.

THE YOUNG WITCH'S GARDEN

A YOUNG WITCH NEEDS A GARDEN. IN YOUR GARDEN YOU CAN grow the plants you will use in your **herb magic** with care, harvest them at the right time, and dry them in bundles that hang around your home.

That home, of course, will look different from witch to witch. After all, not all young witches live in a cottage in the woods. But even if your magic is limited to a corner of your bedroom, it can be just as powerful, and even if your garden is no bigger than a few pots on your windowsill, it is just as magical. However big your garden is, try to grow the following most common magical herbs. (Get a grown-up to help you gather and plant the seeds or seedlings.)

CALENDULA. Calendula, or marigold, will thank you for each flower you take, pushing to give you more. Cut the stem of each flower head down at the base of the leaves, harvesting in the early morning before the dew begins to dry. Pinch off each flower and allow it to dry in a basket, keeping it out of direct sunlight. This may take longer than you expect—give it two weeks, just to be safe. Leave a few seeds for next season, of course!

CHAMOMILE. The most magical part of this plant is the flower, and you'll want to wait until it is at its peak to harvest it. When the sun is high in the sky in the late morning, go through your chamomile, looking for a blossom that is *just about* to open. Pinch it off at the base and leave it to dry in a basket, adding more flowers throughout the summer. Be sure to allow a few to go to seed so that your chamomile will continue to grow next year.

LAVENDER. Allow your lavender to come into full bloom, then carefully use a pair of scissors to trim stems three inches or so below the flowers. Do this in the early morning, before the dew has dried. Gather them into a bundle and hang them upside down to dry.

LEMON BALM. Lemon balm can be used fresh a few leaves at a time, or it can be harvested by cutting the stem two inches above the soil before it begins to flower. Bundle and hang upside down to dry.

MINT. Use fresh as often as possible. When your mint starts to get unruly, cut it down to one inch above the ground just before it flowers. Tie the stems and hang them upside down to dry, or freeze them.

MUGWORT. This should be harvested right as the plant begins to flower, before the blossoms open completely. Remove the leaves and flower heads and dry them separately on paper-lined trays. Do not hang them to dry!

MULLEIN. You can use mullein fresh, or you can dry just a few leaves at a time on a cloth for a plant's first year. By the second year it will be hardy enough to harvest the leaves by cutting the thickest stems close to the base of the stalk, bundling and hanging upside down to dry. You can also harvest and dry the flowers and buds for similar use.

ROSEMARY. You can use fresh sprigs throughout most of the year, as rosemary is fairly hardy even in cold weather. To harvest, collect sprigs about three inches from the top of the plant, just as they start to bloom. Tie and hang these upside down to dry.

SAGE. Use this fresh a few leaves at a time. To harvest for drying, take the maturest stems just before they go to seed, cutting them right down at the base of the plant. Lay your stems in the same direction and tie them tightly together with string. Hang them upside down to dry for at least a week.

THYME. Thyme can always be used fresh, but it grows so rapidly that harvesting is usually necessary. Harvest your thyme midmorning, cutting near the base of the plant just below a new branch filled with healthy leaves. Bundle and hang to dry.

VERVAIN, BLUE. Vervain should be allowed to flower for a few days before it is harvested. Both the leaves and the flowers should be harvested; trim the vervain as you would thyme and pinch off the flowers to dry separately as you would marigold or chamomile.

YARROW. Harvest your yarrow after the flowers are in full bloom, cutting the entire stem halfway down the plant. Bundle and dry hanging upside down out of direct sunlight.

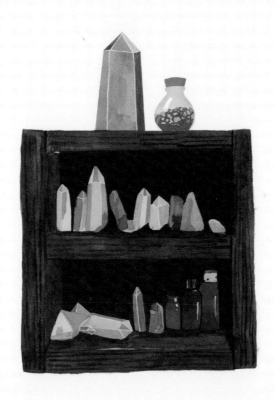

THE YOUNG WITCH'S CUPBOARD

THERE ARE SEVERAL ITEMS THAT ARE ALWAYS USEFUL TO HAVE
on hand for working everyday magic. You don't need a cauldron like witches in
books have, but a decent-size pot is a good tool. In fact, you'll need two, since
you don't want to make balms for your skin in the same saucepan you use to
brew tea. You'll also need one **mortar and pestle** to grind and mix the edible
herbs you'll be using. You'll need a good selection of jars, spray bottles, and
containers, including some of those dark blue or brown glass bottles for storing
tinctures and essential oil blends. Ask a grown-up to help you find these at
health food stores or online.

Crystals

There are a *lot* of powerful crystals out there, and part of the way you grow as a witch is by getting to know which crystals work best for you. These stones are a good place to start in your magical journey to witchy wellness, and again they can be found online or at witchy supply stores. You'll see some of these crystals are associated with *chakras*. If that is a new word for you, don't worry, we'll talk about these next.

AMETHYST. This opens your crown chakra, connecting you with the mystical unknown. It helps with meditation, calm, and tranquility and relieves headaches.

AQUAMARINE. This opens your throat chakra, helping you express your personal truth, and it also calms fear and tension.

CALCITE. Calcite makes your energy more powerful, allowing you to communicate with the spiritual world.

CLEAR QUARTZ. You could have clear quartz and that's all, if you wanted, because clear quartz does pretty much whatever you need it to as long as you simply focus your intentions. If you leave clear quartz as is, it will serve as a general healing stone.

HEMATITE. This is a protective stone, and it will ground you and help you feel safe.

LAPIS LAZULI. This is a powerful stone to help you focus. It will also help with meditation.

OPAL. Opal also makes your energy stronger and adds creativity to your magical life.

Your crystals will need to be **cleared** and **charged** every so often, depending on how regularly you use them. To clear your stone, you can rinse it in wild running water, such as a stream or rain, or you can simply soak it in salt water. You can also leave it out to rest in moonlight or sunlight, as some crystals don't like to get wet.

Charging your crystal can be as simple as holding it while focusing your intention for it, but if you have a little more time, you can perform the following ritual.

Stand in pure light—sunlight if you're looking for clarity, moonlight if you're looking for mystery—and cup your crystal in your hands so that the light shines upon it. Set your intention for the stone, speaking it aloud or in your mind, and then hold it to your heart, as you bow your head and give thanks.

Chakras

A **chakra** is an energy center in the body. Picture a chakra as a wheel or swirl found in specific places along your spine. There are seven main chakras, and when they are open and balanced, the mind, body, and spirit are whole and connected.

MULADHARA (Moolah-dhah-ruh). The **root chakra** is found at the base of the spine. It is the most basic of all chakras, giving you your connection with the past, your ancestral memories, and your deepest link with the earth. It responds to the color red and with stones associated with safety, like hematite, red jasper, or garnet.

SVADISTHANA (Svah-dhis-thah-nuh). The **sacral chakra** is right above the root chakra, just below your belly button, and it is the source of your creativity and imagination. It responds to orange stones like citrine or carnelian.

MANIPURA (Muh-ni-pooh-ruh). The **solar plexus chakra** is just above the belly button, and it represents your inner strength and confidence. Bright as the sun, manipura responds to yellow jasper, pyrite, or the powerful tigereye.

ANAHATA (Uh-nah-huh-tuh). The **heart chakra** is in the center of your chest, and it links together all the other chakras, keeping them in balance. It represents all kinds of love. Anahata is traditionally green colored and responds to malachite and rose quartz.

VISHUDDHA (Vee-shood-huh). The **throat chakra** is found right at the base of the throat, and it's about speaking the truth and standing up for what you believe in. Its color is light blue, like aquamarine or turquoise.

AJNA (Aahj-nyuh). The **third eye chakra** is found right between your eyebrows, and it helps you see things clearly, including the experiences and emotions of other people and of yourself. Its indigo nature responds best to stones like lapis lazuli and azurite.

SAHASRARA (Suh-hus-rah-rah). The **crown chakra** is found at the very top of the head, and this magical chakra helps you find and use your **intuition.** This deep purple chakra responds best to amethyst or clear bright stones like clear quartz or selenite.

Essential Oils for Wellness

Essential oils are liquids that are the purest form of the healing plants you will use. That means a drop of spearmint essential oil, for example, is more powerful than a fresh spearmint leaf. Again, there are a *lot* of essential oils out there, from a wide variety of sources that can vary in quality. There's no need to buy the really expensive stuff, just make sure what you get is 100 percent undiluted—and definitely don't drink it! Even essential oils made from herbs you normally eat, like sage or thyme, can be poisonous because they are so strong. Also some essential oils are so concentrated they may irritate the skin—the notes that follow will mention the ones that are safe on skin. Make sure an adult helps you handle essential oils until you really get the hang of using them.

You'll want to investigate which essential oils work best for you and your magic, but here are a few to get you started.

CHAMOMILE. This gentle oil is useful for skin care (it's safe to apply directly to your skin), bugbites, and helping you feel calmer.

CLOVE. This powerful oil is good for your lungs and digestion.

GINGER. This is warming and energetic.

LAVENDER. The ultimate in soothing and relaxing essential oils, lavender is safe on the skin and can be used to reduce headaches, help with sleep, and restore emotional balance.

LEMON. It's not such a great idea to use lemon directly on your skin, as it can lead to sunburns, but its healing and energizing powers can work wonders when blended with another oil, like olive or almond oil.

PEPPERMINT. This gives your heart, mind, and lungs a burst of energy.

ROSE. This is as good for your skin as it is for your heart. It offers a sense of calm optimism.

SWEET ORANGE. This is the happiest of all essential oils. It provides comfort and a sense of well-being.

The
MAGICAL WELLNESS
INSIDE YOU

. . . .

EVERYTHING YOU DO IN THE WORLD STARTS WITH DECIDING you can do it—and that's true of magic, too! In order to become truly powerful, you need to grow your own personal strength. This section has rituals, spells, and recipes that all work toward the same goal—to make your personal power stronger. You'll start with healing, move on to soothing, and finally reach empowering—for it is only when you are healed, calm, and open that you can find the source of your power.

Warning: you'll be drinking *a lot* of tea.

HEALING
MAGIC

YOUR TEA RITUAL

MANY CULTURES IN ASIA PRACTICE TEA CEREMONIES. IN CHINA, the act of making tea for someone else shows respect, gratitude, or even an apology, while in Japan, the ceremony begins with a ritual purification or cleaning. Everything from examining the teacup to where you place your lips to take your first sip is done with very specific intentions.

Doing something as simple as drinking a cup of tea can have meaning, making it more than just a beverage. And the *kind* of tea you drink matters, as different teas cause different responses in your body. Most of the teas you'll be making in this book are loose-leaf blends. But for your tea ritual, you can use a bag of tea you got from the store or anything else you like!

Before you brew a cup of tea, wash your face and hands so that you come into your ritual free and clean of all that has happened to you throughout the day. Put your water on to boil. While the water is heating, close your eyes and take three deep, cleansing breaths.

Choose your mug with care. This may seem silly, but it does matter. Do you want something comforting, like a chipped mug that has been around for as long as you can remember? Do you want something beautiful and inspiring, like a china teacup? Do you want a mug with a silly slogan or one that refers to a TV show or book you love? Choose the mug that feels right for this cup of tea and in this moment.

When your water is boiling, turn the heat off. Allow it to rest until the bubbles have stopped. Ready your tea strainer with whatever tea you want or need today or put your tea bag into your cup. Slowly, with a steady stream of water approximately six inches above the rim, fill your cup with water. Let the tea steep, and if you like, you can use this time for meditation, for deep breathing, or even for simple daydreaming. (Black teas are usually steeped for three minutes and herbal teas for a little longer. Check the instructions for the type of tea you choose.)

When your tea is ready, remove the strainer and bring the cup to your face. Close your eyes. Inhale deeply three times. Focus your intention for this cup of tea and what it will bring you. Then, take your first sip.

If you want, continue drinking with intention and thoughtfulness, focusing on the moment. But you can also just go sit down on the couch with a good book, text a friend you haven't talked to in a while, or anything else that feels good and nourishing for you.

AYURVEDIC TEA

AYURVEDA IS A HEALING SYSTEM DEVELOPED IN INDIA THOU-sands of years ago. The term means "the science of life," and it is based on the understanding that the mind and body are deeply connected. So if the mind is nourished well, it can heal the body. You can nourish your mind through meditation—which is like relaxing your mind and body—through getting good rest and exercise, and with specific herbal remedies. Ayurvedic tradition employs thousands of herbs. This particular tea uses some herbs that help connect the mind with the body—which will get rid of your stress:

○ Ashwaganda   ○ Brahmi or gotu kola   ○ Jatamansi (spikenard)

These three herbs are both calming and balancing. Ashwaganda will reduce cortisol (a stress hormone) in your brain. Brahmi (or gotu kola) helps the brain get rid of anything harmful to it. And jatamansi (also known as spikenard) helps you feel calm and happy. These herbs are all available for order online, or you can find them at health food stores.

   None of these herbs, however, taste that good, but you can make them taste better with the addition of other equally healing herbs. These are usually easier to find and have a yummier flavor:

- Cinnamon
- Holy basil
- Cardamom
- Clove
- Gingerroot
- Turmeric

Cinnamon makes your brain work better. Holy basil is deeply calming. Cardamom, clove, and gingerroot all help with your body's blood circulation and your stomach's digestion. And turmeric reduces stress.

You can make a tea using any combination of the listed herbs, choosing whatever you can find easily. You'll want to keep the herbs as fresh and close to whole as possible and use twice as many good-tasting herbs as the not-so-great-tasting ones.

Here are a few tips for brewing tea with certain herbs: If you're using ginger, slice it up first, asking for help from an adult if you need it, and don't worry about peeling it. Add all your ingredients to a mortar and pestle and crush them together, splitting open your cardamom pods and breaking down your cinnamon sticks, using the wetness of the ginger to bring life to any dried herbs you have. You'll want a total of about a half cup of blended herbs. Take notes about what you use and how much of each ingredient, as every person's body and mind are different and will react differently to the herb combinations. You'll want to pay attention and adjust your recipe until you've found the perfect blend just for you.

Bring two quarts of water to a boil. With intention, add your chosen ingredients and stir them clockwise for clarity. Lower the heat to a simmer, cover the saucepan, and let your tea brew for at least 30 minutes. (You can let it brew for as long as two or three hours, too.)

Once your tea is done brewing, pour the liquid through a strainer or cheesecloth into a jar or pitcher. This will help keep all the little bits of herbs out of your tea. The tea can be enjoyed both hot or cold and is delicious if you sweeten it with a little honey and milk.

SAD DAY BREAD

EVERYONE HAS SAD DAYS. WHETHER YOU'VE HAD A FIGHT WITH someone you love, a disappointment, or a feeling like you messed up on a test or in sports, it's important to know that everyone feels this kind of heavy sadness once in a while. Of course, these feelings don't last, but knowing that doesn't necessarily help at the time. Sometimes the only way to get through these emotions is to allow yourself to feel them fully. You might not always let your emotions in—instead, you may try to turn away from feeling sad or frustrated. This doesn't usually work well and instead might leave you stuck with those sad feelings for longer than you need.

Letting yourself feel your emotions—especially bad ones—isn't easy, though. You have to *decide* to do it. The ritual of making and eating this bread can help you with that.

INGREDIENTS

½ teaspoon
dried marjoram

½ teaspoon dried sage

½ teaspoon dried
garlic powder

1½ teaspoons
kosher salt

1½ cups very
warm water

1½ teaspoons honey

1½ teaspoons
active dry yeast

3 cups bread flour,
plus a little more
for kneading

1½ tablespoons
olive oil

Begin by combining your herbs with your salt. Grind them in your mortar and pestle, breaking them down and mixing them together. Remind yourself that marjoram is for grief. Sage is for clarity. Garlic is for protection. Salt is for protection, purification, and blessing, and it is the ingredient that will bind them all together.

Add the warm water to a large bowl. Stir in your honey, and then sprinkle the mixture with yeast. Allow the yeast five minutes to activate. During this time, add your herbs to your flour in a separate bowl, making sure the herbs are evenly mixed in. Stir the flour mixture into the bowl of yeasty water using a wooden spoon. Add the olive oil. Stir 21 times—seven and three are both very powerful numbers—in a clockwise direction to help you see your own emotions.

Cover your bowl with a dishcloth and allow it to rest for one and a half hours, or until it is twice as big as it started. While the dough is rising, find a way to pass the time. Maybe you can write in a journal or meditate or spend some time outdoors. Do whatever helps you feel your emotions and begin to let them go. When the hour and a half is up, sprinkle some flour on your counter or tabletop, and lift the dough onto your flour. It will be fluffy and sticky. Knead your dough seven times—and put your heart into this. With each fold and press of your fist into the dough, release any anger, any sadness, any hurt. Punch it into the dough. When you're done, gently

(continues)

and lovingly fold your dough into a nice round shape and carefully place it on a baking sheet covered in parchment paper.

Leave your dough on the counter and let it rise for another hour. Spend that time doing something that feels good and healing for you. When the time is up, heat the oven to 450°F, and let the dough continue to rise for another half hour. Just before putting it into the oven, flick the dough with water three times. Bake for 25 to 30 minutes, or until the bread sounds hollow when you knock on it gently with your fist.

When it's done, remove it from the oven and let it rest on a cooling rack for five minutes, so the bottom remains firm. Slice thickly, and eat warm, spread with butter and honey. You have put your heart into this bread—now take it back into yourself, for it is yours and it is whole. As you eat each piece, feel the sadness or other heavy emotions float away.

CRYSTAL CHAKRA RITUAL

THIS RITUAL IS FOCUSED ON OPENING YOUR CHAKRAS, THE seven points of energy in your body, and bringing them into balance with each other. Begin by giving yourself time, peace, and quiet. Find a ritual space that works for you—this can be your bedroom, the floor, a patch of grass outside, anywhere you can lie flat—but make sure it feels calm. You can turn on a soft night-light or play some gentle music—follow your instincts here! Gather a selection of stones, one for each chakra, and see page XVI for ideas of which crystals work best with each chakra. Take a moment to set an intention for each crystal so that it resonates with its assigned chakra, then set a timer for 15 to 20 minutes.

Lie flat on your back and begin to place your crystals: Starting at the crown chakra, hold your stone to the top of your head for the space of a long breath, then place it on the floor an inch or so above your head. Moving to the third eye chakra, place your stone right on your third eye. Place your throat, heart, and solar plexus chakra stones where they belong on your body and place your sacral chakra stone just below your belly button. Hold your root chakra stone in the open palm of your nondominant hand. Close your eyes.

Lie still, breathing deeply and evenly, as you allow the crystals to come into harmony with your chakras and with each other. You may feel your body and your emotions responding to certain chakras.

When your timer goes off, don't get up right away. Come back to your body and to your present moment, but do it slowly, allowing yourself to make the journey with ease and care. Remove your stones in the reverse order that you placed them. Take one last deep breath and release it before opening your eyes.

SOOTHING
MAGIC

LAVENDER
CHAMOMILE
CUPCAKES

CUPCAKES ARE DELICIOUS—AND THEY CAN EVEN CALM YOUR soul. These dainty, pretty little things can warm your heart and make you smile. That in and of itself is deeply magical and deeply important. These cupcakes are a gift you can give to yourself—and anyone else who might be in need of them.

INGREDIENTS FOR CUPCAKES

1 teaspoon dried chamomile

1 teaspoon vanilla extract

2 cups flour

2 teaspoons baking powder

½ teaspoon salt

1 cup milk

½ cup butter, at room temperature

¾ cup sugar

2 eggs

The day before you plan to make these cupcakes, grind your chamomile into a fine powder using your mortar and pestle. Sprinkle the vanilla extract over your chamomile. (The alcohol will help the chamomile to infuse its flavor into the liquid, but don't worry, all the alcohol will burn off as the cupcakes bake.) Pour into a small jar and let the mixture steep overnight. If you can, surround it with moonstone and amethyst, and leave it in a place where the morning light will warm it slightly.

When you're ready to make your cupcakes, begin by preheating your oven to 375°F. Line a muffin tin with paper liner cups. Mix your flour, baking powder, and salt together using a wooden spoon, stirring in a clockwise direction. Pour your chamomile-vanilla solution into the measuring cup containing your milk.

Using an electric or stand mixer, begin by blending your butter and sugar together until it is light and fluffy—usually three to five minutes. Beat in your eggs one at a time. Then, add half a cup of the flour mixture and blend. Add a quarter cup of your milk mixture and blend. Keep following those steps until all the ingredients are well mixed.

Pour your batter into the prepared muffin tin and bake for 18 minutes, or until golden brown. Remove the cupcakes from the tin and allow them to cool while you make the frosting.

(continues)

INGREDIENTS FOR FROSTING

2 cups powdered sugar

⅓ cup hot water

3 tablespoons fresh or dried lavender flowers

2 large egg whites, at room temperature

½ teaspoon cream of tartar

¼ teaspoon salt

Begin by making a lavender simple syrup. Whisk together your powdered sugar, hot water, and lavender in a saucepan and raise the heat until it boils. Allow it to boil for one minute, whisking constantly, then remove from the heat. Strain out the lavender and set the syrup aside for a bit.

Using a clean and completely dry electric or stand mixer, mix the egg whites together with the cream of tartar and salt at high speed. Slowly pour in the hot simple syrup in a small stream. When it has all been added, continue to beat at a high speed until a nice, spreadable consistency has been reached.

By now the cupcakes should be cool enough to frost, but double-check them just in case. Spread the frosting generously and decorate with lavender or chamomile flowers if you have them. Share the cupcakes with your friends and loved ones, but make sure to eat just one by yourself, sitting with a cup of tea and allowing yourself this sweet, soothing gift.

ELDERBERRY SYRUP

ELDERBERRY SYRUP IS A VERY OLD REMEDY THAT WORKS WELL to heal the body. Lemon and honey together can be very healing, as they blend vitamin C and antibacterial effects in a soothing way. Mullein and yarrow both help to heal coughs, sore throats, and fevers, while elderberry makes your immune system stronger. It also helps treat both sinus infections and allergies.

INGREDIENTS

1¼ cups purified water

½ cup dried elderberries or 1 cup fresh (*Sambucus nigra* variety)

1 teaspoon dried mullein or 1 tablespoon fresh

1 teaspoon dried yarrow or 1 tablespoon fresh

¼ cup raw honey

¼ cup fresh lemon juice

If you're using fresh herbs and berries, collect them by moonlight or in the early morning. If you're using dried herbs, mix them together, then sprinkle them over a bowl containing aquamarine or turquoise and let them sit in sunlight or near a dim light for at least an hour to boost their healing powers.

Fill a pot with water, then let it rest in the sun for at least 10 minutes before putting it on the stove to boil. Place clear quartz, garnet, or obsidian crystals nearby on the counter if you can.

Once you bring the water to a boil, simmer the berries and herbs for 30 minutes or so. Keep an eye on the water, as you don't want the pot to run dry—you can always add a little more water if you need to. Pour the liquid through a strainer and let it cool before stirring in the honey and lemon juice.

You can add this syrup into hot water or tea or simply take it by the spoonful to cure a cold. It will keep in the refrigerator for a month or two.

GENTLE REST TEA

DO YOU SOMETIMES HAVE TROUBLE FALLING ASLEEP? YOU CAN help yourself so you can sleep better by doing a few things, such as meditation or exercise. Sometimes, though, sleep still isn't easy. If you are having trouble, talk to an adult, and then think about making this cup of tea right before bedtime—when you're already in your pjs but you haven't brushed your teeth yet.

Set a small pot of water on the stove to boil. If there's a moon out, mix your herbs in her light, using a combination of catnip, lemon balm, valerian, yarrow, and vervain—you only need a teaspoon in total for just one cup of tea. Add this to a tea strainer and pour your just-boiled water over it. Allow it to steep for at least 10 minutes. While you wait, spend time journaling or reading—definitely stay away from devices like phones or televisions. Keep the lights as dim as you can without straining your eyes. When your tea is ready, sip it slowly, as you continue reading or journaling. Don't rush to finish and hurry to sleep; instead, start early enough so that you have time to really relax into this moment. When your eyes start to feel heavy, move slowly through brushing your teeth, saying goodnight, and climbing into bed—that special place for comfort and rest.

CRYSTAL LOVE RITUAL

THERE ARE SO MANY DIFFERENT KINDS OF LOVE. YOU FEEL love for yourself, for your family, and for your friends. You love the earth and peace and nature. Love is the most powerful force a person can know, the source of all that is good and right in this world.

But somehow, sometimes it's hard to really *feel* all that love. You might not always notice the love other people give you or the love you have to give—though both kinds are always there. This ritual is here to help you open up to all types of love. You'll need only two crystals for this ritual: malachite and rose quartz. Malachite will open up your heart chakra, allowing love to flow in and out, and rose quartz will focus that love. Before the ritual begins, take a moment to infuse your rose quartz with your intentions for the kind of love you want to give and receive.

You will need about 15 minutes to perform this ritual. Try to find a quiet, restful space to do this in. Maybe you'll want to diffuse some essential oils, like ylang-ylang, rose, jasmine, or sandalwood. Set a timer for 10 minutes.

Lie flat on your back, either on the floor or on your bed, and try to roll your shoulder blades under you so that your chest feels open to the ceiling. Place your malachite crystal at the center of your chest, right over your heart chakra, then hold your rose quartz in your nondominant hand. Close your eyes.

Inhale through your nose, breathing deeply so that you feel the malachite rise and fall, but also smoothly so that it doesn't roll off of your chest. As you inhale, gently squeeze the rose quartz. Then, open your palm up to the sky as you exhale, letting the crystal rest in your hand. Keep breathing, allowing any fear or frustration or anger you've been experiencing to empty into your crystals. You don't even have to think about what you've been angry about or anything like that—just allow your breathing to pull those emotions out of you, letting them go.

When your timer goes off, let your breathing come back to normal. Remove your stones and sit up slowly. Take one last deep breath.

Before you use your stones again, make sure you cleanse them of the energy they have taken on by letting them rest in moonlight or sunlight, helping them get all clean and refreshed for the next time you need them.

LOVE AND FRIENDSHIP TEA

SINCE LOVE IS SO POWERFUL AND SO IMPORTANT, IT'S A GOOD idea to have several different spells handy to help you focus on love, especially for your friends. Like the crystal love ritual, this tea ritual can help you feel love, but it does so by working on the balance of emotions inside you. There are a lot of herbs that can help you feel love for yourself, your friends, and your family, so here are several options you can choose from depending on what you need:

BASIL helps you feel love in your daily life.

CARAWAY protects the love that is already in your life.

CARDAMOM invites courage in friendship.

DILL helps you sense and feel the love around you.

LEMON BALM helps you find soothing and comforting love.

VANILLA brings forth sweet and generous friendship.

You'll want a teaspoon's worth of dried herbs, or a quarter cup's worth of fresh herbs, for this tea. If you're using fresh herbs, chop them up a bit so you can release their juices and help them blend together. If you're using dried herbs, gently grind and mix them together in your mortar and pestle. Add your herbs to your tea strainer and pour just-boiled water over them, allowing them to steep for 10 minutes. Enjoy with milk and honey, and remember this sweet, calm, loving warmth the next time you feel a little lonely or shy. You are loved.

A SOOTHING MEDITATION
FOR YOUNG WITCHES

MEDITATION IS NOT EASY. SOMETIMES, WHEN YOU THINK about meditation, you may ask yourself: "Am I actually meditating now? How about now?" It seems like you're supposed to be completely free and not thinking at all, and it's common to get upset with yourself when you can't stop thinking—which of course only makes you more stressed and less able to meditate. The truth is, people are *always* thinking, even when they are meditating, and the key is to let the thoughts come and go without worrying about them.

Sometimes even that feels too hard, though, and when that happens, it can be helpful to try a guided meditation, which can keep you focused and not distracted by every idea that flits across your mind. Controlling the breath, which is also known as *pranayama*, can really help to calm the chatter of a busy mind. Meditative music can also drown out any distracting noises, whether they come from the real world around you or from inside your own head.

The purpose of this particular meditation is to soothe you and to help you learn how to find peace within yourself. Begin by rubbing lavender, chamomile, or sweet orange essential oil on the soles of your feet, where your pores are the most open. Sit *comfortably*—you can lie down or relax against a pillow and even snuggle up under a blanket to get cozy.

Take your index fingers and gently close the flaps over the opening of your ears (these are called the *tragus*). It'll probably feel like you're plugging your ears against the outside world—and you are! Allow your eyes to close, but don't force them if they don't want to be shut. Breathe in deeply through your nose, listening to how loud it sounds with your ears closed. When you breathe out, give a little low hum, like a bee buzzing. This pranayama is called Bhramari, the Humming Bee Breath, and it tunes out all outside distractions, helping you find a space within yourself. You can keep breathing in this way for as long as you like, stopping when you feel calm and peaceful. If you want to, you can keep resting in silence, knowing that you can always come back to this quiet place inside yourself whenever you need to.

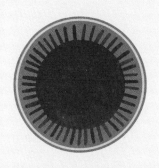

EMPOWERING
MAGIC

BRIGHTENING BREAKFAST BARS

YOU PROBABLY ALREADY KNOW HOW IMPORTANT BREAKFAST is—it gives you the energy you need to wake up and sets you up to have a positive and healthy day. But sometimes people eat breakfast too quickly and without paying much attention to it because they are in a hurry to get on with the day. Maybe you are rushing to school or camp or simply gobbling down a bowl of cereal to get out the door. If you need a speedy breakfast, these bars are quick to eat but still bring a bit of healthy magic to your mornings. They contain oregano, an herb that calms stress, which allows you to feel clear-eyed and energetic instead of overwhelmed. These bars also include ginger, a natural energy-booster; cinnamon, which improves brain function; pumpkin seeds, which are full of vitamins; and dried cranberries, which help your blood flow smoothly and boost the immune system. Think of them as a portable, solid potion that will energize and focus you as you face the challenges of your day.

INGREDIENTS

2 cups oats

½ teaspoon salt

½ cup packed
brown sugar

½ teaspoon
ground ginger

¼ teaspoon
ground cinnamon

¼ teaspoon
dried oregano

½ cup dried
cranberries

½ cup pumpkin seeds

2 tablespoons
chia seeds

¼ cup honey

6 tablespoons
melted butter

When you have some time—maybe on a Sunday afternoon—preheat your oven to 350°F. Line a nine-by-nine-inch baking pan with a sheet of parchment paper, and rub some extra butter on the paper and the sides of the pan.

Begin by grinding ⅓ cup of oats in a blender or food processer until they are fine and powdery. Pour them into a large mixing bowl, and add the rest of the oats and the salt, sugar, herbs, berries, and seeds. Mix them clockwise with a wooden spoon.

In a separate bowl, mix the honey with the melted butter and a tablespoon of warm water, whisking clockwise. Pour the wet ingredients into the dry ones and mix them with your hands, clumping and crumbling. Put some energy into this—energy that the bars will give back to you when you eat them in the morning. Pour your mixture into the prepared baking pan, pressing it into place.

Bake for 30 to 40 minutes, or until the mixture is getting a bit golden. They won't have set completely, and that's fine. Allow the bars to cool for about 20 minutes, then use the parchment paper to lift them out of the pan. Place them in the refrigerator for another 20 minutes.

At this point, the mixture will have set enough to cut into bars, though you'll probably want to ask an adult for some help as cutting them can be a little tricky. Store them in the refrigerator, and they will make a quick and ready breakfast—but when you eat them, take a moment to enjoy tasting them, feeling the energy they give before you go rushing off into your day.

DIVINATION TEA

YOU CAN NEVER KNOW THE FUTURE—NOT REALLY. AND PER-haps that isn't a bad thing. This tea won't give you the answers to an upcoming test or tell you whether the sun will be shining during soccer tryouts. What it *can* do is help you to look inside yourself, to figure out what is true *for you*. It can tell you whether a new friend you've made is likely someone you will want to keep in your life or whether you should call the friend who moved away that you haven't talked to for a long time.

Now, **divination**—the act of looking within—needs some help from you. You can't just drink this tea and expect all the answers to be given to you. You need to put in the effort and look deep. This tea will help with that process, but nothing and no one can do it for you.

This tea is best consumed at night, and even better if on the night of a full moon. Set a small pot of water to boil, and mix one teaspoon's worth of the following herbs:

YARROW. An herb with a long history and a lot of magical and healing properties, yarrow will help you see further and more clearly.

ROSEMARY. This is said to be for remembrance, but along with improving your memory, it also helps your brain function, so that you can understand what you see.

MARIGOLD. This can help you see what is hidden.

LAVENDER. This peaceful herb gives you clarity and boosts your imagination.

Press the juices out of your herbs in a mortar and pestle, and then add them to your tea strainer. Once your water has boiled, allow it to come to rest. When all the bubbles have stopped, pour the water over your herbs, and let them steep for five minutes.

Sip your tea slowly. Try not to do anything else while you drink—don't read, don't look at a phone or watch television, don't chat with friends or family. Just sit quietly, in the moonlight or some other low light, and ask yourself these tough questions: "What do I want? What makes me happy? What do I want to bring into the world, and what do I want the world to bring to me?"

HOW TO READ TEA LEAVES

THE ART OF READING TEA LEAVES—WHICH IS ALSO KNOWN AS **tasseography**—is hundreds of years old. You do it by looking for certain shapes in the tea leaves, like when you find shapes in clouds. Certain shapes in the tea leaves have meanings. For instance, here is a list of some standard symbols and their interpretations.

APPLE. You'll have good health and good fortune.

BIRD. You'll discover new information and decisions that need to be made.

BOOK. You'll have more learning.

BUTTERFLY. Expect happiness and exploration.

CLAW. You'll experience negativity or gossip.

CROSS. There's a challenge to be overcome.

CUP. There is an opportunity awaiting you.

DRAGON. Expect a sudden and enormous change.

EGG. You'll have new ideas and new plans.

EYE. You'll find strength or solutions to problems.

HORSESHOE. You'll have good fortune.

HOURGLASS. This is a sign that you shouldn't wait.

KEY. Expect things are going to get better.

KNIFE. This is a sign of hard times, particularly in friendships.

PALM TREE. You'll find honor, fame, and wealth.

RAVEN. Note that a change is coming, but it's probably a bad change—or might seem so at first.

TOADSTOOL. This is a warning against gossiping or taking chances.

There are a *lot* of symbols you might see in your tea leaves, but this list gives you an idea of the way tasseography works: an image comes to mean something cultural—like the way we think snakes are evil—and that cultural understanding is how you interpret your leaves. Now, if you are reading for yourself or someone you know well, then you might have a little more information that can help make your reading truer—like a snake representing your dad who loves reptiles, or something like that.

To perform a reading on yourself or someone else, use a shallow white teacup with a saucer or a small plate, as this will allow a greater space for the leaves to settle and let you see the shapes more clearly. Brew whatever kind of tea will best help give you the answers you seek, but add the water directly to the herbs, without using a strainer. Be sure to use small, dried herbs, as they will form clearer pictures. Allow your tea to steep for five minutes, and then drink the tea, leaving a teaspoon or so of liquid behind, along with the floating herbs.

Swirl the remaining tea in your cup three times. Quickly flip the teacup over and place it upside down on the saucer. Spin the cup three more times as it rests on the saucer, then turn it back over. You will probably find a bunch of different pictures in the herbs. Use their different meanings along with where they show up on the cup to understand the full reading. The handle of the cup represents the self—yourself or the person you are reading for. The rim of the cup represents the present. The sides show events in the near future, and the bottom of the cup is the distant future.

Reading tea leaves requires you to use your imagination and your intuition. You might feel awkward or silly doing it at first, but if you trust your instincts and go with the flow, tasseography can be a useful and fun form of divination.

PSYCHIC POWER OIL

THIS OIL IS USEFUL FOR WHEN YOU'RE NOT QUITE SURE WHAT you want or when you're feeling a little lost and confused. It will help you understand yourself. Mugwort is an herb with a long history. In Norse mythology, it is one of the nine herbs of power used by the god Odin. Yarrow supports your divination and psychic abilities. Anise will give off a sweet scent, making your energy more positive so that you can see good things. Mint invites positivity and makes things clearer. Note: a little of this balm goes a very long way.

INGREDIENTS

1 tablespoon dried mugwort or a quarter cup fresh

1 tablespoon dried yarrow or a quarter cup fresh

1 tablespoon dried anise or a quarter cup fresh

1 tablespoon dried mint or a quarter cup fresh

Carrier oil like olive or almond oil

Jar

If you're using fresh herbs, collect them by the full moon and make the oil that same night. If you're using dry or a combination, mix the dried herbs together and sprinkle them over a bowl that contains lapis lazuli, opal, and calcite. Charge them overnight on the night just before the full moon.

On the night of the full moon, chop your fresh herbs finely, and then mix all herbs together in a mortar and pestle, breaking them down as much as possible. Place them in a jar and then cover them with the **carrier oil**. Allow the tincture to rest for one month, in darkness during the day and in moonlight at night when possible, shaking occasionally.

In the light of the next full moon, strain into a dark glass container, where it will keep for months. You likely will not need more than a teaspoon at a time to bring more power to your spellwork or meditations—you can either sip it or use it to anoint your temples or the soles of your feet.

MOON MANIFESTATION RITUAL

THE MOON SHINES WITH THE LIGHT IT RECEIVES FROM THE sun. The moon's light can be so powerful that it casts shadows on the ground and so bright that sometimes you can almost read by it. The moon is so influential that it can control the water in the oceans throughout the day and night. What effect can this bright, powerful orb have on you?

Even though the rhythms of the moon are mysterious, you can still use them to add power to things you want to have happen in your life—something known as **manifestation**. Each phase of the moon's cycle brings its own power. The following ritual takes you through an entire **lunar cycle**, and all you need to complete it is a pen, paper, and a curious mind.

The Waxing Crescent

That tiny sliver—the start of new growth—brings with it a sense of possibility. On this night, journal or write on pieces of paper the things you most want to grow in your life, whether that's creativity, success, adventure—anything! Use your imagination.

The Waxing Moon

As the moon grows, your possibilities grow with her—but unlike the moon, these possibilities don't just happen on their own. If, for instance, you want to grow up to be a writer, write every day, even if it's just a few sentences. Do the work to make your dreams come true.

The Full Moon

This is your moment of power and clarity. If you have felt for the past two weeks like you have been working in the dark, now you'll be able to see where you're going—and what might have been holding you back.

The Waning Moon

You should continue to work toward your dreams here, but with all the new information you received from the full moon, you'll be able to work even better. Don't be afraid to take a risk.

The Dark Moon

On this night, we have only the light from within to guide us. Look deep inside. Are you on the right path? What has this month brought you? What have *you* brought to this month? The moon's cycle is about to begin again, and that means new possibilities are coming. Maybe you want to dream something different this time around.

The MAGICAL WELLNESS OUTSIDE YOU

. . . .

YOU'VE DONE A LOT OF WORK TO TAKE CARE OF YOURSELF ON the inside. It is the most important place to start—but it is only the beginning.

We are all affected by things that go on around us, too. A rock can scrape your knees. A harsh word can scrape your heart. A thunderstorm can startle or thrill you. You can't stop these things from happening or from having an effect on you. But you can change how you respond to them. If something good happens, can you find a way to really enjoy it? And if something bad happens, can you still find joy?

Doing this kind of work is magical, but it means that you need to pay attention to yourself, making sure you have what you require to be happy, healthy, and in a positive state of mind.

HEALING
MAGIC

A SORE MUSCLE POULTICE

SOMETIMES YOU MAY SLEEP "WRONG" AND GET A SORE NECK, or maybe you are tired from too much exercise or after-school sports. You work your body hard, and that means you might need extra care when you're dealing with sore muscles.

A **poultice** is any sort of hot, soft, moist mass that can be put on a sore muscle to help it feel better. Fun fact: a long time ago, onion and mustard poultices would be placed on your chest to loosen congested mucus if you had a cold. Sounds pretty gross, right?

This poultice doesn't use onions or mustard, and it's very easy to make. Arnica, one of the ingredients, can reduce swelling in a sore area, while comfrey helps relieve pain. Salt will reduce inflammation, while black pepper and/or clove will promote healing.

INGREDIENTS

¼ cup Epsom salts

1 teaspoon arnica oil or 2 tablespoons dried arnica leaves

1 teaspoon comfrey oil or 2 tablespoons dried comfrey leaves

10–20 drops of black pepper or clove essential oil, or a combination

Mix the ingredients with just enough hot water to hold them all together. Because you're in pain, or you're making this for someone else who is in pain, there isn't a lot of time for performing a ritual, so instead, put your intentions and your wishes for help and healing into your work as you assemble the poultice. When it's ready, spread the poultice directly onto the painful area—but only if the skin is unbroken. If you have a cut, even a small one, it's best to place a clean cotton cloth between the skin and the poultice. Allow the mixture to cool and dry, and then gently remove it.

EUCALYPTUS HERBAL OIL

EUCALYPTUS HAS A LONG TRADITION OF HEALING, PARTICU-larly in Australian Aboriginal practices. It stimulates mucous membranes and clears the lungs, helping you breathe better. You can create this **herbal oil** ahead of time and store it for when you have a nasty chest cold.

The juniper used in this recipe is good for protection, purification, and healing. Both juniper and eucalyptus bring the growth, power, and reliability found in their trees.

INGREDIENTS

4 ounces eucalyptus leaves, fresh or dried

1 ounce juniper berries, fresh or dried

Carrier oil like olive or almond oil

Small jar

If you're using fresh eucalyptus leaves and fresh juniper berries, collect them in early to midmorning on a bright clear day. Chop them finely. If you're using dried leaves and berries, sprinkle them over a bowl containing turquoise and clear quartz. Allow them to sit in the sunshine for an hour.

Mix your ingredients in your mortar and pestle, bruising them and bringing them together. Place them in a small jar and cover them with your carrier oil. Allow them to rest in sunlight for six weeks, then when they are finished steeping, you can use the oil when you need to. Just rub a little over your chest or beneath your nose to ease your breathing and to help your mind feel clearer. Store your oil in a cool, dark place, and it will keep for at least a year.

AYURVEDIC MASSAGE OIL

ONE OF THE MANY TRADITIONS OF AYURVEDA IS REGULAR massage, also known as Bahya Snehana. Sesame oil is traditional in Ayurvedic medicine, but you can use another oil like sweet almond or avocado oil. The ginger you add will stimulate your muscles. Turmeric will help your joints move smoothly, and cardamom will reduce any swelling, while giving you a feeling of comfort and well-being.

INGREDIENTS

3 ounces sesame oil

10 drops ginger essential oil

10 drops turmeric essential oil

10 drops cardamom essential oil

Dark glass jar or bottle

Mix all the ingredients well, and store in a dark glass jar or bottle, allowing them to rest at least a week in a dark space. If you can, surround the bottle with yellow jasper, pyrite, jade, and citrine. When it's ready, massage the oil into your feet, onto your scalp, or over your entire body, focusing on your joints, like your elbows, wrists, ankles, and knees. Follow the massage by adding heat to your body by taking either a hot bath or a hot shower. If you can, rest for the remainder of the day, allowing the benefits of your massage to seep into your body.

YOGA MASSAGE

YOUR INTERNAL ORGANS NEED LOVE AND HEALING, TOO, BUT they're a little harder to get at than your skin! So **yoga** can be a massage for your body from the inside out. If you're not familiar with yoga, don't worry—these five poses are really simple. Together they will wring out your system like you're wringing out a wet towel, loosening up anything that might be blocked inside and making you feel stronger and calmer.

Paschimottanasana
(SEATED FORWARD FOLD)

Start by sitting on the floor with your legs stretched out in front of you, pointing your toes to the sky. Sit up as straight as you can. Dig your heels into the ground and bend your knees slightly. Raise your arms straight up overhead and reach them forward past your feet, grabbing onto the outer edges of your feet if you can reach them. Take a deep breath in, and as you exhale, lower your forehead to your knees. If you feel comfortable doing so, straighten your legs. Stay here for three breaths.

Ardha Matsyendrasana
(SEATED SPINAL TWIST)

Sit with your legs stretched out in front of you with your spine straight. Lift your right leg and cross it over your left, bringing your right foot over by your left thigh and keeping your right knee pointed up to the sky. Keep your left toes pointing toward the sky, too. Hook your left elbow around your right knee and extend your right hand to the floor behind you to help you keep your balance. Use your left elbow to help move your chest to the right. As you do this, look over your right shoulder. Be gentle with yourself. Stay here for three breaths and then repeat on the other side.

Pavanmuktasana
(WIND-RELIEVING POSE)

Lower yourself onto your back, bringing your knees up to your chest. Wrap your arms around your knees and gently lift your head and chest so that your nose brushes your knees—or gets close to them. Stay here for three breaths.

Supta Matsyendrasana
(RECLINED SPINAL TWIST)

Lower your head and chest, and extend your right leg out long, keeping your left leg tucked into your chest. Use your right arm to bring your left knee over to the right side of your body. Try to keep your right shoulder on the ground while your left knee approaches it. Turn your head to look past your left shoulder. Stay here for three breaths and repeat on the other side.

Setu Bandha Sarvangasana
(BRIDGE POSE)

Lying on your back, bring both knees up so they are pointing to the sky, with the soles of your feet on the ground. Place your palms flat on the ground by your sides, and inhale. As you exhale, lift your hips to the sky, keeping your feet and palms flat. Inhale again, then exhale to release your bottom to the ground. Do this twice.

GENTLE SHAMPOO AND CONDITIONER FOR YOUNG WITCHES

MAKING YOUR OWN SHAMPOO IS SUPER-SIMPLE BECAUSE ALL you need is an inexpensive, gentle soap that is already made and easily found in most stores: liquid castile soap. Castile soap is made with a vegetable-based oil, rather than animal fat. The most popular brand is Dr. Bronner's, but there are others that an adult can help you find. This homemade shampoo will be thinner and runnier than you might be used to and won't suds up nearly as much, but it is a gentler approach to healthy hair—and it's better for the environment.

Shampoo

You'll want to make your shampoo based on what kind of hair you have. (If you need to, ask an adult to help you decide this.)

DRY HAIR

- Chamomile
- Aloe
- Calendula/marigold
- Peppermint

OILY HAIR

- Rosemary
- Lemongrass
- Ginger
- Lemon peel

If you shower or bathe at night, begin your work in the evening, and if you shower or bathe in the morning, start in the morning. Collect a quarter cup of herbs (you can use fresh or dried). Bring one cup of water to a boil and pour it over your herbs. Allow herbal water to steep overnight surrounded by moonstone, amethyst, and rose quartz or throughout the day, using sunstone, aquamarine, and pyrite.

INGREDIENTS

1 cup herbal water (as made above)

1 cup of castile soap

2 tablespoons vegetable glycerin

2 teaspoons argan oil

80 drops of essential oils that match the herbs you're using

1 tablespoon aloe vera gel

Strain your water into a mixing bowl. Add the remaining ingredients. Mix well and pour into an empty shampoo bottle. Use just as you would store-bought shampoo.

Conditioner

Making conditioner is a lot like making shampoo. Brew your herbal water using the same ingredients that you did for shampoo, then add it to a spray bottle, along with two tablespoons apple cider vinegar (*not* the raw kind, which would clog the sprayer) and about 40 more drops of your essential oil blend. The vinegar will balance the pH of your hair, reducing frizz, and will detangle it as well.

After shampooing, spray the conditioner onto your hair and let it sit for a few minutes before rinsing; don't worry, the vinegar scent won't last once your hair is dry.

Every once in a while—once a month if you have oily hair or twice a month if your hair is dry—give yourself a hair oil treatment following these instructions.

INGREDIENTS FOR DRY HAIR

2 tablespoons olive oil

2 tablespoons argan oil

5 drops essential oils of your chosen blend

INGREDIENTS FOR OILY HAIR

2 tablespoons olive oil

2 tablespoons jojoba oil

5 drops essential oils of your chosen blend

Mix all the ingredients together in a bowl, then rub and massage the oil into your hair, paying special attention to the ends. Leave the oil in for half an hour. Sit in the sun if you can, allowing its warmth to help the oils be absorbed into your hair, then take a shower and shampoo your hair. You can also add just a few drops of this oil to your hair every day to help keep it soft.

EARTHING RITUAL FOR WELL-BEING

IT'S IMPORTANT FOR YOU TO TAKE A MOMENT TO GROUND yourself every so often so you can connect with the earth and find your inner peace. For this ritual, all you need is time and intention, but you can boost its power with the following items:

- Hematite crystal—a stone of protection and grounding. You can also use clear quartz, holding it in your palm and setting an intention for it to protect you from negative energy.
- An essential oil blend of sage, lavender, and thyme
- Access to the earth, either dirt or grass. If you can't get outside, don't worry—just sit on the floor.

Start by taking some slow, deep breaths. You might want to dab a little essential oil on your temples and on the soles of your feet. Sit comfortably, as low to the ground as you can. Hold your crystal lightly in your palm and sit with your hands in your lap.

Close your eyes and begin to pay attention to the world around you. Feel the air on your face, the earth (ground or floor) beneath you, the smells and sounds around you. Continue to breathe slowly and deeply.

Really *feel* your connection to the earth. See if you can notice the natural pulse of the earth—her heartbeat—and let your breath come into sync with it. Let your mind drift and continue to breathe.

When you feel ready, allow your eyes to open, slowly and gently. Take a final deep breath and bow your head to your chest. When you rise to your feet, move slowly, feeling the earth beneath you, supporting you.

SOOTHING
MAGIC

PLANTAIN AND HONEY SALVE FOR BRUISES OR INSECT BITES

THE HERB CALLED PLANTAIN IS ACTUALLY A WEED. IT GROWS IN just about every lawn in North America, and people often try to get rid of it. The thing is, it's actually really helpful! It can work to fight off bacteria and reduce swelling and can even help your skin to heal.

Honey is another antibacterial substance, and together with plantain, acts to soothe and protect your skin from cuts, scrapes, stings, and insect bites.

Start by making an herbal oil. Gather enough plantain leaves from your yard or a nearby park to fill a small jar. Wash and dry them, then roughly tear or chop them to release their juices. Cover them with an inch or so of an oil of your choice—coconut oil or olive oil are excellent options for skin care and pain relief. Close the jar and leave it in the sun for at least six weeks. Surround the jar with citrine, garnet, obsidian, pyrite, and turquoise.

INGREDIENTS

¼ cup herbal oil
(as made above)

¼–½ ounce beeswax

1 tablespoon honey

30 drops of
a combination of
chamomile,
helichrysum, lavender,
or patchouli
essential oils

Mason jar

Strain your herbal oil into a small saucepan and heat it at a low temperature. Add ¼ to ½ ounce of beeswax, depending on how soft or firm you want your salve to be. When the beeswax has melted, add the honey and the essential oils, and pour the mixture into your jar to cool. Spread your salve directly onto stings, bites, bruises, and small cuts and be amazed by how well it helps you heal!

RELAXING BATH SALTS

BATH SALTS ARE SO EASY TO MAKE AND HELP RELAX SORE MUS-
cles, reduce swelling, get rid of toxins in your body, and more. What's funny
is that the best kind of salt for your body—Epsom salt—is not actually a "salt"
at all. It's a natural mineral compound of magnesium and sulfate. Baking soda,
another natural mineral compound, also helps get rid of toxins in your body
while healing and soothing your skin.

INGREDIENTS

1 cup Epsom salts

1 cup baking soda

½ cup dried herbs
(roses, calendula,
or lavender)

20–30 drops of an
essential oil blend of
your choice (lavender,
rose, or peppermint)

Mason jar

Blend your Epsom salts and baking soda in a
bowl. Mix in your dried herbs. Add your essential
oils and mix it all together. Store in your jar and use
in your bath every week or so to help cleanse and
heal your body.

HEALING BATH RITUAL

BATHS ARE INCREDIBLY HEALING AND COMFORTING. CULTURES around the world, from Iceland to Japan, look at bathing as a ritual—something that should be done with intention. Baths are seen by many as a chance to be peaceful and to even meditate. You don't need a giant bathtub to enjoy a healing soak; as long as you can immerse yourself in enough water to relax, you've got everything you need.

Of course, it's always nice to add a little extra to your bath! Here is a way to make this ritual even more powerful.

(continues)

INGREDIENTS

1 cup Relaxing Bath Salts (see page 54)

1 sprig each of fresh vervain, rue, lemon balm, and lavender

A glass of water

Soothing music

Let everybody in your family know that you will need at least one hour of alone time. Choose your music, playing it at a low enough volume to allow you to feel calm, but loud enough to mostly drown out the noise from the world around you. (And remember to always keep any device that is plugged in away from your tub!) If there's a lot of stuff, like shampoo bottles or things in your bathtub, clear them out and set them aside. Begin filling up the tub.

Make the bath as hot or cool as you like—if it's summertime, you may not want a hot bath, but in the winter you may want it to be a little steamy. (Test the temperature of the water with your elbow to make sure it's not *too* hot.) As the water flows, add your salts and your herbs. Before you get in, lean over the tub, stirring the water counterclockwise. While you stir, set your intention for this bath. How will you feel during the ritual? How will you feel afterward? If you can, speak these intentions aloud, so that the vibrations from your voice go into the water. When you are ready, step carefully into the tub and settle in.

Now, just be present in your bath. Sip water from your glass. Splash your fingers a bit. Close your eyes. Spend as much or as little time in the bath as you want. Let your body and mind relax as much as possible.

When you feel ready, step out carefully. Allow the tub to drain, and fish out any petals or herbs floating in the water.

SWEET DREAMS BALM FOR A GOOD NIGHT'S SLEEP

IF YOU LOVE BEING IMAGINATIVE OR IF YOU ARE SOMEONE who is empathetic (that means you might be affected by the energies or emotions of other people), you might sometimes experience nightmares. Nightmares are actually *really* important—they are a way for your mind to work out all the worries you've been struggling with. But it's also important to get a good night's rest, so if you've been having nightmares too often, try using this balm to bring yourself sweet dreams instead. Note: you'll want to make this in advance since it needs to sit for a few weeks before you can use it.

INGREDIENTS

¼ cup herbal oil

¼ ounce beeswax, grated

15 drops lavender essential oil

10 drops sweet orange essential oil

Mason jar

Create an herbal oil, as you did in the Plantain and Honey Salve on page 52, with a scent you find calming and peaceful. If you have one already made, use that, or you can put together a new one with a vanilla bean, sweetgrass, or lemon peel—or any scent that feels good and comforting to you. Let it sit in sunlight for six weeks, surrounded by amethyst, lapis lazuli, moonstone, and rose quartz.

Once the oil is ready, heat a quarter cup of the oil over very low heat until you can feel the warmth rising. Add the beeswax and stir clockwise until it has melted. Remove from the heat and pour the mixture into your jar. Add your essential oils and stir. Cover and let it set for two hours. At night, rub it gently on your chest and the soles of your feet before you climb into bed.

YIN YOGA PRACTICE FOR YOUNG WITCHES

YIN YOGA IS A TYPE OF YOGA WHERE YOU HOLD STILL IN A pose for a little while, rather than moving quickly from one pose to another. It allows you to grow stronger in a gentler, more peaceful way. The poses here will help your body relax into the stretch, letting gravity do the work for you, so that you can release any stress you might be carrying in your body. Yin yoga will also help you with meditation, as your body gets more used to the idea of being still for a longer period of time.

Sukhasana
(CROSS-LEGGED POSE)

Sukhasana means the "pose of ease," and it's pretty much the way you used to sit criss-cross applesauce on a classroom carpet. Because it's not very comfortable to sit cross-legged for long, try using a pillow or folded towel to sit on, getting your hips a little higher than your knees. Sit up as straight as you can (make the muscles in your stomach tighter so you don't hurt your back), trying to keep your heart in a line over your hips, and your head in a line over your heart. Rest your palms on your knees, using your arms to push you up straighter. Breathe in and lift your chest up to the sky. Stay in this pose, sitting quietly, for at least two minutes.

Salamba Bhujangasana
(SPHINX POSE)

Start by lying on your tummy on the floor. Place your elbows under your shoulders, with your palms flat on the earth. Press into your palms and let your forearms take your weight as you lift up. Keep your chin tucked under, looking down past your nose, so you don't strain your neck. When you breathe in, feel your chest press toward the floor, making you float a little. Stay in this pose for at least two minutes.

Utthita Balasana
(EXTENDED CHILD'S POSE)

Starting on your hands and knees, bring your toes together and spread your knees so that they are wider than your hips. Reach your arms forward and lower your whole body to the earth, bringing your forehead to the ground if you can. Keep your arms stretched and your palms flat, allowing your hips to rest on your feet. You can feel your back stretch as you breathe in. Stay in this pose for at least two minutes.

Eka Pada
(PIGEON POSE)

Starting on your hands and knees, bring your right knee up toward your right wrist, and move your right foot out toward the left of your body. Stretch your left leg out straight behind you, and slowly relax over your bent right knee, lowering onto your forehead if it's comfortable for you. Breathe deeply, feeling your belly press against your right leg when you inhale. Stay in this pose for at least two minutes, and then switch and do the same on the other side.

Supta Baddha Konasana
(RECLINED BOUND ANGLE)

Lie flat on your back and bring the bottoms of your feet together, with your knees pressing out to the sides. Place your palms on your belly and breathe, feeling your belly rise. Don't push your legs down to the earth, but just let gravity help them relax. Stay in this pose for at least two minutes.

WELLNESS WATER RITUAL

CULTURES ALL AROUND THE WORLD BELIEVE THAT WATER IS magic—which makes sense, because you need water to stay alive. But something makes it extra magical. Water gives you a sense of protection, of forgiveness, and of mystery. It holds you up, letting you float in it, and it washes you clean.

For this ritual, you'll want to wait for a rainy day. If you can, hold out for a really drenching rain, not just a light drizzle. Stand in a doorway or open a window on a very rainy day. Extend your palms outside, so you can feel the individual drops of water as they slap and break on your skin—but keep the rest of you dry. Then bow your head and step out fully into the rain. Let it fall on your head and shoulders, massaging you, until water begins to drip down your face. Slowly, with your eyes closed, raise your face to the sky. Open your palms.

Think about what you feel, standing there in the rain. Do you want to run inside and curl up under a blanket to get dry? Do you want to go stomp in some puddles? Follow what you feel and let the water guide you.

EMPOWERING
MAGIC

FINDING YOUR VOICE
LIP BALM

WHEN THE THROAT CHAKRA IS BLOCKED, YOU MAY FEEL LIKE you need to pretend to be someone you are not or to say things you don't really mean. This lip balm will help to open up your throat chakra and let you live with joy and pride. And you can also never have enough lip balm!

INGREDIENTS

1–2 teaspoons beeswax

2 teaspoons coconut oil

2 teaspoons shea butter

Small jar or tin

Over very low heat, melt the beeswax, coconut oil, and shea butter. You will want to use more beeswax if you live in a warmer climate and less if your house stays cool. Gently stir to the right until the oils are well-blended. Remove from the heat. Carefully pour the mixture into your small jar or tin. Let it cool, surrounded by turquoise or aquamarine stones. Use it anytime, especially when you need to have a tough conversation or simply want to have the confidence to speak up a little louder.

THE FIVE RITES

THE FIVE RITES ARE A SERIES OF MOVEMENTS FROM TIBET, DATing back 2,500 years. This is more of a workout than the other yoga poses you've learned so far, and it'll help you get stronger and have more stamina and flexibility. It will also energize you to think more clearly and feel more confident.

And don't forget: between each rite, stand up straight and take two deep breaths.

The First Rite

While standing, stretch out your arms into a T-shape. Spin around, with your arms out like a helicopter, as fast as you can until you become dizzy. (Be sure to do this in a space where you won't bump into any sharp corners or break anything fragile.)

The Second Rite

Lie down flat on the ground on your back, placing your hands palm down next to your hips. Raise your legs up into the air, toes to the ceiling, legs as straight as you can make them. Lift up your head and shoulders but try not to crunch your neck. Stay there for a breath, then slowly lower your feet, shoulders, and head to the floor. Stay there for a breath, allowing your body to relax completely. Repeat this motion five times.

The Third Rite

Kneel down on the ground, curling your toes under you to help with your balance. Placing your palms against your thighs, lean forward, reaching your nose toward your belly. Stay there for a breath. Then lift back up and arch your upper back, pointing your nose to the ceiling. Stay there for a breath and repeat this motion five times.

The Fourth Rite

Sit on the ground with your legs straight out in front of you, toes to the sky and palms flat on the earth beside you. Lower your chin to your chest. Stay there for a breath, then bend your knees as you pull your hips up toward the sky, keeping your arms straight and dropping your head back toward the earth. Stay there for a breath, then lower back down. Repeat this motion five times.

The Fifth Rite

This rite involves moving back and forth from two yoga poses called Downward Dog and Upward Dog. Begin in a downward-facing V-shape with your hands and feet on the ground, arms and legs straight, with your hips up in the air. Take a deep breath. Lower your hips, pulling your chest between your arms and arching your chest up to the sky as your feet curl so that the tops of your feet and your hands are the only parts of your body touching the ground. Take another deep breath and repeat this motion five times.

LOVE AND BE LOVED
BODY CREAM

CHOCOLATE MAKES US FEEL BOTH GOOD AND LOVED. THE PRI-
mary ingredient in this body cream is cocoa butter, which retains a bit of
chocolate's scent, along with its loving, healing properties. Cardamom, clove,
cinnamon, ginger, caraway, and rose will also help you feel love, both for yourself and for the people around you. Don't use all those scents in one batch of
cream, though. You should choose which smell the best to you! You can use
this cream every day to soothe dry skin.

INGREDIENTS

½ cup cocoa butter

¼ cup coconut oil

¼ cup avocado oil

30 drops total of your chosen essential oil blend selected from cardamom, clove, cinnamon, ginger, caraway, or rose

Wide-mouthed jar

Melt the cocoa butter and coconut oil over very low heat. Stir clockwise just until they're blended. Remove your pot from the heat. Pour the mixture into a wide-mouthed jar and mix in your avocado oil and essential oils. Refrigerate for three to four hours, or until the mixture has started to thicken.

Using a stand or hand mixer, whip the mixture on high for 10 minutes. Pour it back into your wide-mouthed jar and refrigerate for another three to four hours. It won't need to be kept in the refrigerator after this; however, if the temperature in your house rises above 75°F, you may need to chill and rewhip the cream.

The MAGICAL WELLNESS IN YOUR HOME

YOUR HOME HAS A BIG IMPACT ON YOU AS A PERSON. YOUR house is the place where you can feel safe and where you can recharge your energy, growing more powerful. The home is the heart of any young witch's practice. It is the source of all that you do. The practices, spells, and trinkets described in this section of the book will help to transform your home into a place that will protect, renew, and purify you.

HEALING MAGIC

FRESH CLEANING SPRAY

SOMETIMES WE NEED TO CLEAR THE AIR. ESPECIALLY IF IT'S been a few days in a row of rain or snow, our rooms can feel a little stuffy, a little stuck. This all-natural and effective spray will boot out the old and make room for the new, all while leaving your room smelling airy and bright. You can use it to wipe up any spills (whoops!) and clear away any stuck energy.

INGREDIENTS

1 cup distilled white vinegar

4 strips of lemon peel

2 cups water

20 drops tea tree essential oil

20 drops lemon essential oil

20 drops peppermint essential oil

Dark glass spray bottle

Heat the vinegar until it just simmers, then add the lemon peel. Allow this to simmer for 10 minutes, then remove the lemon peel and allow the vinegar to cool to room temperature, surrounded by turquoise, obsidian, and clear quartz. Stir in the remaining ingredients and pour into your spray bottle. You can use this to clean your bedroom furniture, your bathroom, or even just to spritz in the air to give it a fresh scent.

BELLS ON YOUR DOOR

YOU MAY BE FAMILIAR WITH HEARING BELLS JINGLE WHEN YOU open a door at a store, the sound letting everyone know that a customer has entered. But bells on doors have been around for a long time, and in fact, they used to be known as witches' bells. The sound bells make can remind you that you are crossing over the threshold of your home or room—welcoming you in or sending you out with energy and good wishes.

Any set of bells with a sound you enjoy will do to hang on your door. Or you can also create your own following these steps!

(continues)

MATERIALS NEEDED

Oven-bake clay

Paint or gloss for oven-bake clay (optional)

Thin hemp cord

Small or medium-size craft bells

Start by molding your clay into a bell shape. One block should be enough for one bell, or for two smaller bells. They do not need to be perfect! Rounded, square, a little wiggly—have fun with it! As you work with the clay, and as you create your shapes and designs, keep your mind on your intentions and your wishes for what energy the bells will send out. When the bells chime, those wishes will come back to you.

Smooth out the seams in the clay and use a pencil or your fingernail to add etchings or designs onto your bells. Make a hole at the top of each of your bells.

Bake them according to the manufacturer's instructions and allow them to cool completely. Use paint or gloss to add stripes or other designs if you like.

When your paint is dry, cut about 12 inches' worth of cord and knot one end of it onto your craft bell. Draw the cord through your clay bell or bells.

Hang them over your door so each time you enter or exit, they jingle.

A SWEEPING SPELL

SWEEPING CAN BE A PRETTY ANNOYING CHORE, MOSTLY BECAUSE it feels kind of pointless. The moment you've finished, you sit down to eat and crumbs fall on the floor again, or dirt is tracked in, the cat sheds, or dust blows in from an open window. And that is *always* going to be true, because you continue to *live* in your home, and life is always a little messy.

But at the same time, sweeping can also be so satisfying, like when you look at all that *stuff* that fills a dustpan or when you feel a clean floor beneath your bare feet. Sweeping is simple, but also powerful. After all, what is more valuable to a witch than her broom?

To connect with the power of sweeping, try not to think of it as another pointless chore. Instead, think about what you are sweeping up. It's not just dust and crumbs and pet hair—it's also old energy that's been lying around.

Start at the outside edges of the room and work clockwise, sweeping toward the center of the room. When you've finally collected your pile in the center of the room, wave your palm over it, magicking away any unwelcome energy that you have gathered. Then—throw all that stuff away.

(A friendly note: If you drop your broom, make a wish before picking it up. You never know what will happen.)

SOOTHING MAGIC

YOUR OWN CRYSTAL GRID

A SINGLE CRYSTAL IS POWERFUL ON ITS OWN. BUT A CRYSTAL'S power can be made much stronger when it is connected with other crystals in a geometric pattern called a **crystal grid**. The following grid will welcome peace and protection into your house and family:

- Clear quartz
- Hematite
- Moonstone
- Obsidian
- Pyrite
- Smoky quartz

You can use any combination of the listed stones, but you will need anywhere between 18 and 36 total. (Tip: three is a magical number, so use a multiple of three.) You will need one quartz point, as well—that's a clear quartz crystal in a wand shape.

Have some fun arranging your crystals, like you're laying out a puzzle. Think about balancing how you organize them. Don't group all the dark-colored stones together. Instead, place a light-colored crystal in between each dark-colored one. The same goes for size. Make sure small stones are next to large stones, keeping the whole grid looking even and pretty.

When your grid is complete, take a moment to give it some of your energy. Starting from the outside and working your way toward the center, use your quartz point to draw lines connecting each crystal. This will help them to work together better to bring protection and peace to your home.

Your crystal grid can be as large or small as you like, and you can leave it up for anywhere from an hour to a month, depending on how much space you have and what you need from it. Crystal grids are useful ways to invite fresh energy and creativity, so build a new one whenever you feel the need!

A RESTFUL SLEEP CHARM BAG

YOUR BODY NEEDS REST, BUT SOMETIMES GETTING TO SLEEP can be hard. You might lie awake, feeling nervous or scared. Well, this **charm bag** will help you be calmer as you go to bed each night. You can keep the bag beside your pillow, or you could even hold it while you drift off to sleep, breathing in its soothing and relaxing scent.

INGREDIENTS

1 tablespoon dried vervain

1 tablespoon dried lavender

1 tablespoon dried yarrow

1 tablespoon dried lemon balm or catnip

Small amethyst crystal (This is good for a gentle and restful sleep.)

Small cloth bag

Stir your herbs together and let them charge in the light of a full moon overnight. Gather everything into a small cloth bag and place it lovingly at your side as you prepare for bedtime. Change it out every full moon to keep the scent fresh and the herbs powerful.

MAGICAL WIND CHIMES

ON DAYS WHEN YOUR HOME'S WINDOWS CAN BE OPEN, THE breeze that might blow through the house can bring with it all kinds of good, cleansing energy. Sometimes we get so busy, though, that we don't really stop to notice when a cleansing breeze is sweeping around us. Wind chimes can remind us to pause for a moment and feel nature's power. And you can make your own wind chimes, which will bring extra powerful good energy to your house. Whenever we craft something with our own two hands, we are pouring out our own special magic into it, making it ours.

Start by collecting different items that you can easily find inside or outside. Some things you could collect might be shells, driftwood, mysterious keys that don't seem to open any of your doors, pretty beads, parts of broken necklaces, or parts of a lost pair of earrings. You want to look for anything that sparks your interest and imagination.

Now look for something to be the top of your wind chime. This can be a piece of wood, an embroidery hoop, or even a big tin can lid. Select the kind of material you want to use to hang your items—fishing line, twine, leather cording, or thin chains. You can attach the string or other hanging material to your top piece with superglue, hot glue, or even just knot them in place, depending on what you use. Finally, arrange your found items so that you have a few on each strand or just one per strand.

Hang your wind chimes in your house or outside your home where you can see as well as hear them when the wind gently blows. Smile each time you notice the noise they make, remembering how peaceful your home really is.

DIY DIFFUSER FOR STRESS

SURROUNDING YOURSELF WITH A SOOTHING, RESTFUL SCENT can reduce your stress from school, extracurricular activities, or family almost immediately—and it's so easy to make your own diffuser with a few supplies from a craft store and some essential oils.

INGREDIENTS

⅓ cup unscented carrier oil, like almond oil or grapeseed oil

Glass bottle or jar with a narrow opening (available at craft stores)

1 tablespoon isopropyl alcohol

10 drops lavender essential oil

10 drops chamomile essential oil

10 drops rose essential oil

3–6 rattan reeds (available at craft stores)

Add your carrier oil to the glass bottle or jar, then thin it with the isopropyl alcohol. Add your essential oils and place the reeds in the bottle, stirring them slightly. Allow an hour or two for the oils to move up through the reeds. After that, you should have a lovely, calming scent that will last for days or weeks.

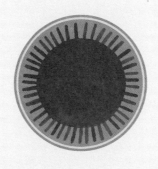

EMPOWERING
MAGIC

THE YOUNG WITCH'S ALTAR

EVERY WITCH SHOULD HAVE AN **ALTAR**. AN ALTAR SERVES AS A place to focus your thoughts and is the center of your magical practice.

Every witch's altar, however, is different, because every witch is different. As you build your altar, think about what's important to you and remember that your altar can always change—because you will change as you grow.

You'll want to keep your altar somewhere private and out of the way, so no one in your family can mess with it. Many witches keep their altar in a corner of their bedroom, or on a dresser or bookshelf. It doesn't have to take up a lot of room, but it should be in a place just for you to use.

Here are some items you may want to include, organized to incorporate the power of the four **elements** of fire, air, water, and earth in your altar. This will invite all the complementary powers of our world to work together in your sacred space.

FIRE	AIR	WATER	EARTH
Volcanic stone	Feather	Seashell	Bowl of dirt
Spices like cinnamon or pepper	Diffuser (see how to make your own on page 85)	Jar of rainwater	Horn or bone from an animal
	Wind chimes (see how to make your own on page 83)	Empty cup	Sedimentary rock

Pick something to place in the center of your altar, like a picture of someone you love or a powerful crystal or even a small bowl. From there, add anything you like around that one item. You can place stones or essential oils on your altar, along with things that you find, like lost keys or shells or pieces of driftwood. Every time the season changes, you should take a look at your altar and see if it needs any changing, too.

RUNES FOR WELLNESS

RUNES ARE AN ALPHABET OR *FUTHARK* FROM A WRITING SYS-tem used by ancient Germanic peoples. Runes can also be used for divination, protection, and other forms of magic. The word *rune* in fact translates to "holding a secret," as runes were believed to be so powerful they could only be understood by the wisest and bravest people.

You can buy runes online or at magical stores, but as always, the most powerful magical objects are the ones you make yourself.

There are 24 runes in the Elder Futhark, and they can be combined to create deeper, more complicated meanings:

FEHU
Luck, energy

THURISAZ
Chaos,
destruction

RAIDHO
Adventure,
leadership

URUZ
Health, strength,
willpower

ANSUZ
Intelligence,
communication

KENAZ
Knowledge,
creativity

GEBO
Balance, generosity,
gratitude

NAUTHIZ
Work, necessity,
life lessons

EIHWAZ
Wisdom, mysteries
of life and death

WUNJO
Joy, happiness,
harmony

ISA
Stillness, concentration,
being stuck in
one place

PERTHRO
Fate, luck,
prophecy

HAGALAZ
Crisis, fate

JERA
Harvest, seasons,
peace

ALGIZ
Protection

SOWILO

The soul, confidence

EHWAZ

Harmony, cooperation,
friendship

INGUZ

Personal growth,
earth

TIWAZ

Justice, sacrifice

MANNAZ

Thoughtfulness

DAGAZ

The link between
day and night

BERKANO

Secrecy, healing

LAGUZ

Water, life, dreams,
imagination, emotion

OTHALA

Household, family,
ancestry

One example of how to use runes is to combine them to create charms. To create a charm for creativity, you could combine Kenaz and Laguz, like so:

Or you could combine Uruz, Jera, Wunjo, and Ehwaz for a rune of peace and happiness:

Which runes speak to you and what kind of charms can you make with them?

Another way to use runes is to make a set to use for divination. To make your own runic stones, gather 24 or more smooth, rounded stones. You can use river stones, quartz, beach stones—whatever feels right to you and that you can find easily. Give your stones a good scrubbing with soap and hot water and let them dry completely. Wipe them down with rubbing alcohol to make sure they're completely free of dirt. Using a permanent marker, draw one rune on each of the stones. You'll want to use a black marker for lighter stones, and a gold or white marker for darker stones.

Allow your stones to dry for 24 hours in a place where both sunlight and moonlight will shine over them. After that, line a baking sheet with foil and bake the stones at 200°F for about 30 minutes. Return them to their drying place and let them rest for another 24 hours before using.

Pull out your runes when you're feeling a little lost, like you don't know what you want to do next. Begin by holding whatever container you are keeping your runes in close to your heart and ask them a question if you have one. It could be, "What would help me feel calm?" or "What do I want to do today?"

When you're ready, reach into the container and pull out a handful of stones—it doesn't matter how many, just grab whatever you can. Toss them gently onto the floor in front of you. If any runes land upside down, set them aside. Take a look at the runes that are faceup. What do they tell you? What answers do they give? How do their meanings work together?

There are no right answers here—it's all about listening to your heart as you read the stones.

DIY PRAYER FLAGS

TIBETAN PRAYER FLAGS ARE COLORED RECTANGULAR CLOTHS that are strung on a line together. They are traditionally used to bless the surrounding countryside or home, inviting peace and wisdom. Even if Bon or Tibetan Buddhism is not part of your heritage, you can take inspiration from this tradition and create your own flags to make your home more peaceful.

You'll need about a yard of white cotton or linen fabric, some sharp scissors, and a needle and thread. Cut the fabric into six-by-nine-inch rectangles. There's no need to hem the fabric or anything—a little fraying is totally fine. Fold the top of the rectangle down by half an inch and sew it down (ask an adult for help doing this if you don't know how to sew), creating a tube for the flag to hang by. Make as many flags as you like, depending on where you want to hang them.

Ask yourself the question: "What kind of magic do I want to use?" You could use thread magic to sew on some runes. Or you could use the power of nature and paint leaves and ferns with fabric paint, using them like a stamp to add to your flags. You could even buy some printable fabric to hang up some of your favorite images or quotes. You could sew on some buttons or ribbons, using the colors of the chakras.

Once you've finished decorating your flags, thread some yarn or cord through them, tying knots at each end of each flag to keep them evenly spaced. Hang your flags up inside your bedroom or in your home to bring you peace and wisdom all year.

THE MAGIC IN YOURSELF

I HOPE THIS BOOK HAS HELPED YOU FIND THE MAGIC ALL around you and given you the tools to imbue your daily life with energy and intent. As you continue your journey of practicing wellness magic, remember that this book is only here to get you started. If there's anything you should remember after reading it, it's that magic isn't something you *learn*—it's something you make for yourself.

Your magic is personal to you, because magic works differently for everyone. You may find that you feel more connected to some kinds of magic than others—maybe crystals really work for you or possibly herbs are better. That's good! Figuring out what is right for you *is* magical. Keep exploring, following your own intuition and creativity, and see where your witchery leads you. It's a great adventure and one that you can explore while making yourself feel healthier, calmer, and happier.

Enjoy the journey.

GLOSSARY

ALTAR. A place to honor your craft. It can be small or large and filled with things that have meaning to you.

CARRIER OIL. A neutral oil to act as the base for magically infused oils.

CHAKRAS. Energy centers in your body. There are seven chakras: muladhara (the root chakra), svadisthana (the sacral chakra), manipura (the solar plexus chakra), anahata (the heart chakra), vishuddha (the throat chakra), ajna (the third eye chakra), and sahasrara (the crown chakra).

CHARGE. To fill with a magical energy and intent. For example, we can charge a crystal generally with the energy of sunlight or moonlight as well as with an individual goal by focusing on and speaking that goal to it.

CHARM BAG. Also known as a spell bag, this is a physical representation of the energies of a spell.

CLEAR. To cleanse of magical energy and take back to neutral. If you've charged a crystal with a goal, for example, you should cleanse it of that goal before you use it for something else by washing it in sunlight or moonlight or in wild water.

CRYSTAL GRID. The practice of laying out certain crystals in a geometric way so that they work together for a certain purpose or intention.

DIVINATION. The art of seeing into the future or into something hidden.

ELEMENTS. There are four basic elements in witchcraft: earth, air, fire, and water. Working with them invites the complementary powers of our world into our magic.

HERB MAGIC. The practice of using plants in your craft, often turned to for healing.

HERBAL OIL. Herbs steeped in oil to preserve their scent and magical properties.

INTUITION. An inner knowing or instinct.

LUNAR CYCLE. The full transition of the moon through all its phases, from new moon to full and back again.

MANIFESTATION. This is an idea that can be considered many different ways—in our case, it means the power to make something you want to have happen actually appear in your life.

MORTAR AND PESTLE. A witch's tool used for crushing and mixing herbs.

POULTICE. A soft, moist mass applied when hot to heal the body.

RUNES. An ancient magic symbol system, often used for divination.

TASSEOGRAPHY. The art of reading tea leaves, usually for divination.

WIDDERSHINS. Moving in a left or counterclockwise direction.

YOGA. A series of poses and breathing exercises practiced to gain control of the body and mind.

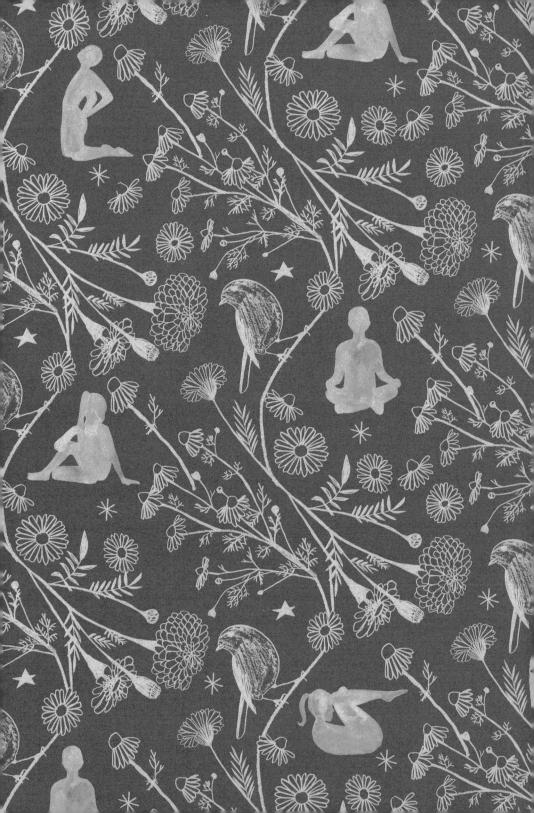